WE ARE ALL WEAK
AND CRAZY WHEN WE
WOULD REPENT

TODD SWIFT

WE ARE ALL WEAK AND CRAZY WHEN WE WOULD REPENT

PEMBROKE POEMS
2017-2018

COMPLETING THE TRILOGY OF

MADNESS & LOVE IN MAIDA VALE

AND *DREAM-BEAUTY-PSYCHO*

First published in 2018
by Eyewear Publishing Ltd
Suite 333, 19-21 Crawford Street
Marylebone, London W1H 1PJ
United Kingdom

Typeset with graphic design by Edwin Smet
Printed in England by Lightning Source
All rights reserved © 2018 Todd Swift

ISBN 978-1-912477-27-2

WWW.EYEWEARPUBLISHING.COM

TO SARA MY WIFE,
AFTER 15 YEARS OF MARRIAGE

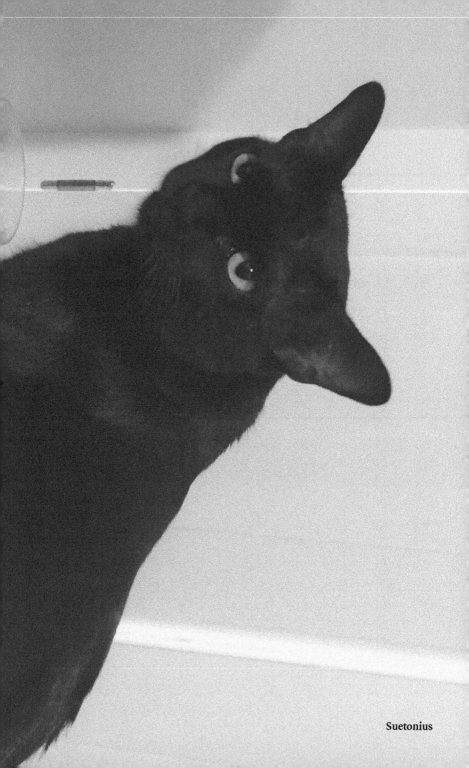

Suetonius

TABLE OF CONTENTS

BRIEF INTRODUCTION

This pamphlet follows those from 2016 and 2017, *Madness & Love in Maida Vale*, and *Dream-Beauty-Psycho*, which aim to chart the spiritual growth, and lack thereof, of a middle-class British husband, turning 50 in the pivotal years of Trump, Brexit, North Korean nukes, ubiquitous porn, Taylor Swift, Instagram, the Bob Dylan Nobel. This is First World anxiety, for better and worse.

It is also about how faith, poetic language, and contemporary culture work together, and don't. It is about guilt and enchantment, despair and profound love; about kindness and a brutal world system. Like any poetry book, it is both personal and well beyond personality. As in my previous books, allusion, homage, stylistic echoes rub against innovation, and disruption. My work is neither traditional or new. It enters a conversation, mid-stream, and tries to jump in as best it can. It is up to the reader to decide whether the poems interlope.

The poems were mainly written during a residency at Pembroke College, Cambridge. The Master, Lord Smith, has been very supportive and enlightening – he is the model of the good person, kind, cultured, generous. I should also like to thank Dr Alex Houen of Pembroke, and Professor Clare Grey. They were intrepid guides. I also wish to thank the porters at Pembroke, all the staff, and my colleagues who made this a good place to be.

I am grateful to Christopher Jackson, of late one of my best readers. And to other incredibly valued poet-friends, whose advice I sought for this pamphlet, and have before: Lisa Pasold, Eric Sigler, and Patrick Chapman. Finally, thank you to Edwin Smet, my good friend, the key designer of the Eyewear look.

Maida Vale, July 13th, 2018

'WE ARE ALL WEAK AND CRAZY WHEN WE WOULD REPENT'
(After a line by Lancelot Andrewes)

For Lord Smith

Between David and Daniel
I cannot find a third fasting,

What's between nothing at all
Until after sundown, and

No flesh to delight our meals?
One's too much of not enough,

The other so fine a cut, it barely
Chastises; no flavouring, just

Sustenance. One's cruel, but a test.
The other's more a sombre jest.

I feel we're meant to stand
Apart from pleasing, but survival

Is allowed. Christ does not want
Sinners in a shroud, just yet.

God expects us to be lean, though,
Sometimes. To be autumnal,

And strip the tree. The puritan
In me enjoys a bare body on a cross.

Nakedness is a form of sacrifice,
After all, or should be. Norms

Have a way of tangling up with thorns.
I'd lie with three or four, any way

And in any gender, if I could,
If the bed's making could withstand

My breaking of the wood with the axe
Of my desire, a heave-ho that cracks

The forests of piety to the rotting heart.
At core, we're in an age of deforestation,

Rangers of bawdiness removing more and more
Covering. This has deviated, in argument if not

Morality, from the sermon he was trying to
Mount, Lancelot, who I like a lot. I was translating

Into my own poetry his sermonic verse – in order
To explore ideas of scarcity, but flourished instead

Into fantasies of ecstasy and sacred plenty – why?
The summer heat – the decaded waves of euphoria.

Once we reimpose the sermon's original aim…
Any food we cannot eat tastes good. What is left

When we renounce the body, ounce by ounce?
Old bread? Stale air? Impounded water? Soup

With a nail that once lifted our saviour bloodily?
Lent lends itself to restraint but also rebellion.

If you ask me to be less than before, you ask
For me to acquiesce or contemplate war.

What of fruit we regretfully ignore? It lies unbidden.
Our reach refuses to achieve what we yearn for.

The grain rots; the silos lonely as the drowning.
The flies despoil the feast outlawed, laid out

On the virgin tablecloth, no wine stains to frenzy
The white flow of the table; smooth and stable,

A sea becalmed by halving rejection. The vermin
Skitter at the foot of the horns of plenty, satiated.

What we hand over the villains have for their own;
Either way, Lent is veal we would be good to spare.

There is nothing fun in what we give on to our Lord;
The point, to kill our appetites, sharpen love's sword.

AFTER MY MOTHER'S THREE-WEEK VISIT

After George Barker

Purely herself,
An enthusiast for Bat Out of Hell
And Windsor Castle,
Beautiful at seventy-five
In shades and a leather jacket,
My mother is to me

More exasperating and remarkable
Than anyone else;
Not only because I am hers,
And she was the one who read me
Frost and Eliot when I was three,
Or because she was a model

Speeding around Montreal
In a red convertible
With my baby form in a shoebox,
Or because she went to LA
And turned down every producer;
Not only for her endless love

For my father, since they met
Skating when she was eighteen;
Not even for the years between,
Sometimes disagreeing
About serial killers, or UFOs;
Not even because of her research

Into family history so we are
Related to Ben Affleck via Knowlton;
Not for her swimming for miles;
Skiing cross-country; her Scrabble
Genius; her effortless kindness
To cats and dogs; indifference

To religions for the most part;
Adoration of Leonard Cohen;
Ability to read novels
Quickly and critically;
More stubborn than any wall;
More determined than any ten

Generals; more sensitive
Than she ever let on,
Except when cooking meals
Designed to flabbergast
Any gastronome; happiest
At home with a fire going,

A blizzard outside; modest,
Braver than Alexander The Great;
Who I love despite all and everything,
Past any laws or limits of reason
Or science, who is my limping
Ageing never-diminished heroine,

Or to be less obviously trite,
I've come to adore my Mary Margaret,
So goodly of a kind is she.
She is like the best apple,
The sun across a just new icicle,
An indelible sharp-right epitaph on stone.

HAIR DYED BLACK

The train to Oxford
goes through Reading

18 year olds no longer
care about what I lack

or possess; special pleading
won't get me off the hook.

I like to quote Mark Ford
and Mark Twain. Never

the twain shall meet.
All aboard! The book train

steams ahead, the living
and the dead off to Newcastle

where the readers are
among their stacked hoard.

Words are years. Are feet.
Measures of the life span

immeasurably harsh to man
and woman. I read in Paris

that God gave Adam a cat
in Eden to ease his burden.

But that is false. A cat
would have pounced

on the snake. Tough break,
that Satan. I am nostalgic

for when my poetry drew
crowds galore. In short

am delusional and grown fat
on the figs of fake fame.

I am a snowfake, snort.
Did drugs in my 20s.

Did wedding bliss in my 30s.
Did PhD and Dad death in 40s.

50s feels like Sisyphus.
Rolling the rock up blueberry hill

is not the same as rock and roll high school.
I have been scolded for being

inappropriately interested
in bodies in devotion.

I am post-Cohen but unforgiven.
Without a guitar poetic smut

sounds smug and exposed.
Music covers a multitude of sins.

Thank you years and nature
and parents and fate, Hume

and Swift, for the broom of a gift,
a tongue tasting verb and noun

despite being a raw wounded thing
that has bled out in search

of renown, like a trapped fox
who bit off a leg to find a life.

POEM ON THE EVE OF HIS 52ND BIRTHDAY

If you are lucky you will live long enough
To experience your 52nd spring

And you will marvel at your irrelevance;
All the young excitements, beyond yourself.

Once you were sixteen, this was new.
You did not know how you would age.

How you would go past your father
When he died. That your body would change,

And what was fresh would become stale.
Memory and clumsy recollections,

The slump and paunch; the decline.
Without a son of your own, no one cares.

Everything is finite. Suddenly 1984
Is not just a novel, but a golden summer.

Despite Reagan and the geo-politics.
Like every other one you want to go back.

There is nothing interesting in this history,
This biological story. It is a simpering complaint.

Get over it. You are not decrepit yet.
There is some chance of a rare interlude.

A brief relapse. Some insight or energy.
A new song, or book. A kiss. A petal.

Sentimentality and a third beer may make
You shed some tears. Recall the engineer

In the Stanley Tavern when you were young
Guzzling the large beer bottles in both hands

Like a man at a teat. Who was he?
The first weeks of April are political,

They remind you that winter was a necessary
Sham, and the dusty shift to a brief better

State is also a temporary measure;
The cycle is endless and tiring.

The old fall, the new march on.
You cannot break out of this with longing

Or song. Language is helpless.
Time is not a disease to be cured.

Until they bring out the super-bodies
That will persist for centuries, this tedious

Narrative, interspersed by grim humour
And relentless panic, will grab at straws,

The drowning that needs music and love,
Sex and narcotics too exhausting

And hard to come by. I am bewildered,
You say, I have been struck by the blank

Side of wonder, this is what being poured out
Is about. I am pour. I am a vessel walking

About the spring day, happy to see blossoms,
Friendly without purpose, suddenly benevolent,

So in love with all that has been taken from me,
And all that is still to be taken away.

WINTER SOLSTICE IN THIRTY LINES

I have no basis, scientific or political
For making claims in language,
Even less religious permission to do so,
Though the Pope has redefined hell
Lately as simply the soul's disappearance,
Which is a comforting diminishment
Of infinite terror in an endless theo-geographical domain,
Since what goes away can return,
As we know reading theory or plays with doors.
And who says lyric expression requires

Any sanction from authority if a revolution?
Statements in this form are their own facts,
Linking uttered imagination to discovery.
To proceed: the solstice intrigues me;
The point of greatest loss a point at which increase begins;
The dying of a glimmer; the fade that cuts
Abruptly to the tomb. In the buried ground
Not much illumination lies around; the sun
Is forgotten, the worms begin their humour,
Their party of sick jokes, the guffaw of rot.

The plot in this cycle is a swing from closer
Planetary alignment, to a less bright position
In the cosmos. Or, less elliptically, the solar
System has an eccentric shape, belying claims
All is perfected – the oval proves the circle false.
The utter abjection of the pit in to which
The disappeared light is thrown today, too early,
Is a happy act, in that soon, incandescence will
Burst the dark dam, huskily crashed open,
Like a bull of light advancing on darkly twisting toreadors.

END OF YEAR BEST OF LIST, 2017

Listening to the LCD Soundsystem comeback,
Which seems a cynical ploy,
But one that paid off, given its position
As top of many end of year polls by critics,

I am struck by how much they sound like
Bowie, New Order and Talking Heads,
But we all knew that, and it is just Eliot's
Tradition and the Individual talent playing out

Again, in a new genre. The canonical
Gets remade endlessly, by artists
Who love the past a little, and try their best
To recreate the sounds that inspired them,

Adding a bit of something original if they can
To the systemic recalibrations.
My list has so much great TV on it,
It is embarrassingly incredible.

Content is king and baby-fisted dictator now.
Dr Sentamu put his collar back on, Kevin S. lost
His weird halo, half of my family is still dead;
And OK Computer turned 20 this year. OMG.

Poetry is political again, as is Depeche Mode,
And poetry became performance poetry again,
And everything was magnified by Twitter,
Like a bitter magnifying glass burning up paper

To send smoke signals. Volcanoes erupt,
And octopi are too smart to eat.
We may live forever with new heads,
Or the plastic seas may swallow us whole.

AN EASTER ANTIBIOTIC

For Christopher Jackson

There is only so much time
In which to consider the infected foot;
And pain is forgotten in time.
I am a bare tree, a bare bulb,

When it comes to Christian imagery
This Easter. I am all out
Of sensational exultations.
I am quietly relieved the world

Is intact; we are all somehow intact.
Walking on eggshells is an image
For the world, this time around.
Christ was nailed to an eggshell.

The fact of the crucifixion is medical
Horror, suffering, and the bleakest
Of moments. But the body is subject
To such shocks. Time jeers at each

Body. Time jeers at our minds, as well.
Our reputations are built on a pinnacle
Of eggshells, blown clean hollow out.
Easter is the spring cleaning

I always ask for, even when I forget
I have been asking. But I have been.
In every hollow bell of my acts,
Each dull wasted moment,

When precisely not suffering a final agony,
I forget what makes any time vital.
That it is breaking open.
That time will break.

I KNEW THE GIRL WITH THE MOST CAKE

Some day you will ache like I ache – Hole, 'Doll Parts'

So, I made the mistake of making a Playlist
That had the songs that comprised my youth;

Or is that compromised, so powerful was I
Addicted to music then, as I am now.

Youth being fancy for under-thirty,
Which is shorthand, still, for being better

Physically, and less sound in the mind.
I suppose I was always kind, but crueller

To my own self, at the time, but in love
With several women who were crueller

Still, but to complain is sexist, and a lie.
We're all foolish fucking in a winter city

Where the beer is cheap and the snow
Piles high for four months each year;

The spring is an exorcism, a revolution
In the blood. Little good comes from

Remembering the kisses and the bareback
Risks, the bisexuality and crack-den jaunts;

It haunts, the pool halls and dealer-girls,
The losing teams, next-day plunging lows.

The strippers who were friends, and those
Who rejected you at orgies for your brother.

The ones who kissed you singing like Monroe,
Because your hair was dyed black-black

And you were thin, weird and sexual.
Or talented and shy. It hardly matters

Who wore the slim tailored suits, or why,
Who used their daddy's tie on wrists or eyes;

Who read the Russians, and who bought
The junk. Who did the taxi driver for sheer fun,

Or spoke of bank jobs as a thrill. Who went on
And off jagged pills, or rouged their nipples,

Or owned a snake as long as a whip.
Or burnt offerings in our basement in a pit.

It's buried now by no one caring one jot.
It was hot that summer, and the bizarre

Love triangles, were, well, hotter.
Then there was the runaway daughter.

Charlatans, Breeders, Pixies, Garbage...
No point in being that age again, professor.

No point is shorthand for saying you can't
Return. Death is worse, but nostalgia is

Not great, either. It's an ache unassuaged
By wit, rhyme, rhetoric or new world wines.

Bit torrent the screeners for Oscar faves,
Brag about missing all the better raves,

Complain you hated Blur, preferred Oasis,
Adored Verve. The guy who nods in the corner

Of the pub, saloon, bar or lounge is you.
The shadowy other, your leaner twin,

A clone who never aged, but nods endlessly,
Like a blow-up clown punching bag creep.

He is doing your exes while you sleep,
He still lives above the flat you painted

Handcuffed to the co-eds from Nebraska.
No asking for a reprieve or approval.

The moral compass of these times has veered,
What you thought was queer in bare factories

And half-ruined lofts is all ramped up now
So far, you appear either irredeemably evil,

Or simply dumb and vile, or even boring,
No different from any pudgy parent in the Tens.

It all depends, but none of your songs are
Destined to open portals to other lands.

You slept with all the ones you chose
Because the ones you wanted were detained

With men taller, more adept at piano
Or sax, and with firmer jaws. The laws

Of desire barely change, or change so fully,
They swing back, eventually. Consider

All the beards we have about us at this stage.
Style, fashion, fickle fame, or fickle dating,

Without apps we had to fend for ourselves,
Pre-digital, in dingy pool halls, using only

Our clothing, reading, and lipstick to entice.
Was it nice to be young in the early 90s?

And by young I really mean, basically thirty.
It was certainly dirty. It was lonely. It looks

Remote. From this vantage it could be a book
High on a shelf, in a vintage shop that has seen

Bigger days. Yes, when the books were owned
By persons of renown, taken down, really read.

SUDDEN JANUARY HAPPINESS, SINCERELY

Start again, start every time,
Start like an Instagram slogan,

Neat, pat, and simple, but near
To what seems true in the dumb

Bone that runs the full length
Of your life like a parent;

Start when it rains, when it runs,
When it shines, when it's brighter

Than dishwater; or dull as dust.
Trust fun, that song of the young,

The inane. It's insane to fear
What catches as catch can.

Eels are sunrays of the deep,
In sleep where I run to bring

My beloved feline home to be safe.
I am thrilled to be glad today.

The nerve of me to be brimful
Of a daylight I can barely see,

But there it is, I am a big believer
In sudden revelations. Start tomorrow

Today, because the slogans end
Eventually. Right now is a good omen

For melting ice, branches budding
In the next quarter, and the rising

Hopes of a whole teen generation
That inventions and discoveries

Will cure everything wrong with
Last year, which is so old, so over me.

I am thrilled to be writing this,
And honoured to be on the page with you.

Thank you words for your sunlight
And your planets. Merci, longer day

For letting me wear your coat home,
And your shiny pin that tells love quotes.

Happy happy happy, it's winter, no joke,
At its thinnest and least wrong, I mean it,

There's a strong breeze of wow this is new;
A whiff of being high-schoolish again, when,

Now, ooh, great, cheers – yes, this is that
Dance you hear about, giddy with no reason

But the senseless cyclotron of its own unwinding,
Devices of joy, turns and twists of gusting devotions.

FOR THE DREAM SYNDICATE IN 2017

We're just guys and dolls
Cruising Highway 61 in a finned Chrysler
Ray-bans blocking out the day's
Cruel ageing, the rusting of youth-zones;
We come out to play at dusk;
Time's husk has left us with something to say;
Diabolical Americana has risen its scythe
And cut down the golden hay; we glide

Effortlessly in the video, older, wiser,
More ingrained. We're indie,
The falls under the modernity of architecture,
The falling away of pain in the needle's gay
Abandon. Power-pop dreaming is a drug-induced
Comma, pausing the blather and rinse-cycle
Our brains get subjected to with TV;
We're better than nothing, barely. But lean,

Gaunt, tall and tanned from having the top down.
We dream and enter your broken town.
Tear the locks off the grain elevators,
Unscrew the lintels from the tombstones.
Grown older, not smarter, we've kept sharper,
Smarting, by going strong, never not touring,
Zombie vampire bats swooping on
To the exposed jugular of the present mediocrity.

Baudelaire. Rimbaud. Tanguy.
Dada. Bauhaus. Velvet undergrounds.
The sounds of difference once were mighty
And stranger in a long and windy land.

We have returned, oppressed not a jot, hot
In our fedoras and suits, LA-tonsured,
Bronzed like pig iron. We'll kiss your mothers,
Date your sisters, and spank your daughters gently

But only with their entire permission.
We're the good vandals, the damned band
Filtered through a surreal passion for love's embers
And the debris of narco-works, lesser soda jerks.
Thin and coming, we drive like a shoal
And reach our lonely goal, a dead-eyed Texaco
Gas station, without pump or purpose,
An icon bleary on a blood-rimmed, angry horizon.

One man's poison is another gal's rock and roll;
Yet all politicians and hangovers take their toll.
Bruise me in the motel, and bruise me after dark.
I hear angels. Hark, I hear the ether.
America's breakers breaking hard
On a broken shore. Burroughs buried here.
We called out for more, more, more
And got more than we bargained for.

ON DECEMBER 2017 COMING

The darkening December almost here
Makes me tender, want to protect

Small creatures from killers,
Who are out there, doing awful things

Because the small are loved carelessly
And left to wander. I need to track

And halt the pet-butchers out there,
As winter approaches, gingerly,

As if testing the year's wound;
It's a time of cuts and bruises,

Falling down stairs; always has been,
Say the comforters, but that's not

A truly comforting appeal to reason.
Without a God, it's monstrously sad,

The opening into bleak mid-winter
Orbiting beyond the window

Like a bully's taunt; with one,
It's merely bafflingly difficult, truly

Agonising, like pulling darts out
Of your arm in a particularly rowdy

Pub after hours in a madhouse storm;
There's a blizzard of loss on the way,

And another has just passed;
Assistance was dropped by plane,

Killed half the population, those
Crushing boxes marked C A R E

Are not too careful when they're thrown;
Cats are kittens full-grown, their brains

Could power most nuclear stations; but
Compared to dolphins, they're not bright;

And compared to Darwin, Newton, no one is light
In the gale, on damaging seas. I shiver

At the encroaching cold, just as I suspect
The fires to come will also instill shivering

Of another kind. The awesome is the awful
Given a different provenance or purpose,

But the laying waste to nations and towns
Is always awe-inspiring and horrific. Ice

Forms on a blade and a skull, no hill
Remains ice-free when the zero falls

On the dead, the living, and those between,
Whose identities are inter-life, interleaved

In the cautious limbo of wanting to save,
To avert harm, but falling short, falling silent.

I'd kill to protect the gentle, the meek, the mild,
That defenceless, ridiculously egg-shell child.

POEM IN LATE SEPTEMBER

It is still September...
that slow month
like a hinge; summer
through the door.
Winter, other side.
If you cried when leaves
abandoned us, you dried
tears when the sun
at today's start appeared –
a dazzling coda,
a comic epilogue in a dark play.
The dog days let out
again into the golder garden,
running the show's hot riot.

September 2017, London

PERVERSION AND THE POET

I have hated myself
For a while now
And will again.
I want to be slim
Like a girl
I loved when I was young.
She ran and jumped into a pool.
Honesty is the best policy
Unless you are hiding something
But I remain in the open
Because what I am is not the worst
Possible thing, I am no child

Killer-lover, no villain
Of uncontrollable arrogance,
The high conceit
Of an education giving
Smart people the license to thrill
Themselves aesthetically;
Only the stupid are authentically bad?
Evil I am not, if I was evil
I would love myself more,
As all evil people love, if even
Just a tad or with artifice, their sins,
Even when, in the mirror

Weeping to delete them
Just before they begin again,
To slither down the ivy,
Raise the portcullis
And scramble into the dark port

With what cannot be translated
Into flesh, without the fuzz
Becoming involved.
I do not plot to contrive
Crimes for my own alternative
Plain of command. No Sweeney,
I am simply a trouble-husband

With the eternal lusts of the imbecile,
Wanting, for a second,
To sup with the devil's concubine
And know problematic contortions
Of the she-monster who wriggles
So well we come eternally,
Like a Jagger impersonator
In Hugh H's Vegas brothel
On Planet Sexualis Prime III.
I am no whipsmart charioteer
In leather and Latin,
Dominating slaves for championship

Adulation in the one percent arena.
No excuse for the precisely vile
Things some men do;
Under red ceilings of charities.
Regrettsville. Pop. 1.
Or universal, everyone.
A broad spectrum from Manson to me,
From Moors maniac to you;
And all that inbetween
Is a sun lounger for awful acts.
I want to surgically remove
My body from my body,

But stay alive,
With a very large thingamybobbin
And also surgical breasts
And a lot of money, billions
Upon billions. It is the wise
And godly who are all sexes,
Beyond definition, sublime
In their openness to possibility
Of satiation in all stations
Along the ways of pleasure.
My tastes are simple, strictly confined
To what is legal if ill-defined,

By church, forbidden only because
Of Jesus vows. But the law allows
Crimes of the heart
That any lover starts, any felon
Knows is usual in precincts
Where the wolf outlasts the dove.
I climb into the ratified air
And am good, so good.
I remain, a virtue not to transform
Into a swarm of cockerspaniels, to
Wreck the holy marriage amid wedding
Wheat. I retreat from sin,

I go back in to good, a bed boy
In the proper bed, made by
The unsolicited over-age maid.
I act my age, I possess rectitude
Like a ram up my butt.
My soul's finishing school

Fell into a Swiss ravine
After a minor avalanche.
I know the way of wisdom
Involves renouncing poetry,
At least the kind of poetry
I tend to write. Desire excites
Self-examination, even milk
Mixing with meat.
Perversion creates by extension
Of the limits of the permissible.
Falls off, and dissipates.
The limping cop in the alley

Is dying of a bloodshot dream.
I was the Christ child
And the whore of all betrayals.
The sea drank up the beach
And choked
Before it could get inland;
Islands are months
Of bleached words,
When nature failed
To be all and end all.
But I could love with time,
With patience.

May 2017

JACK REACHER

We have been married about 15 years, give
Or take a few days, and neither of us
Is Jack Reacher, therefore, we are not
Winners of the lottery of life; our

Fists are not the size of supermarket chickens;
We cannot take out five bikers outside
Their bar, after warning them hospital
Awaits if they don't back down;

We don't know every dogleg backroad
In every buttfug dusty nowhere town;
We can't call the Pentagon by memory
Dialling from a payphone;

And we own a mortgage, lots of clothes;
We drink as much coffee, but use floss
As well as a toothbrush; don't make love
In showers in every book, precisely once;

Because, we are not ex-MPs, and live
Outside Lee Child's universe
Where the military is in decline,
But the men and women in uniform

Are mainly good, except when they step
Out of line, and then justice finds them
In the giant avenging form of a journeyman
Evolved for aeons to break heads and hands;

No, nothing ever goes as planned.
Rule number one in battle, shit hits
The proverbial, and soon enough it's
Incoming this and incoming that,

And the only law is that of friend for friend,
And never leave your men and women behind;
War being shit and blood in the end, and Purple
Hearts, which is another way of saying wounds.

We took a hit when the landmine along our road
Went off, blowing away any chance for a child
Or children we'd wanted; losses in the name
Of love. I can hold you in the morning,

But I cannot smash a trio of sadists to clean
The mess that biology delivered like a missile;
Incoming yes, and afterwards, medalled,
They leave you in a hospital, on your own;

Every married person is a veteran, and the claim
That love is hell, or war, is a tired, but true vehicle.
It is because it means more than what's before
And after. It's the tissue, and the main thing,

The big red one, D-Day, the over the top,
The whistle and then jump; the shooting start;
Only death or betrayal kills the agreement;
War is love, as well, it's all one metaphor;

As Homer knew, because men armed
Hold each other as they bleed out,
As they run or fall; and men hold each other now
As husband to husband, and wife to wife

Also, pleasing to Sappho; we have improved
On the classical poets in our mixtures of the loved;
But in the manner of battle we're declining;
Few heroes murder like a bird removed above

The sand on which their enemy dies;
We spy too much with our satellite-fed drones,
Do more than the gods even once did;
We cry because we are young; but have aged;

That's in the past for Jack Reacher, he's left
His battalion, he does what he does for reasons
Private and lean; probably connected to a fear
Of staying rooted too long in a rootless land.

How do we root ourselves fifteen years on,
My heroine, my commander, my warmate?
Is the ceremony of decision enough, promises
Binding the bones we can barely heal?

It's all sticking up out of skin stuff,
We're tough and tall, but comparatively small
And weak, we break each other too;
We're lovers who fight to love better, ill-equipped,

Therefore human in an inhuman time;
What makes us human is rhyme, it creates
A splint to join shattered words; bodies that fail.
All life is sad, you say – you chose me,

Not fecundity, not a big family. We have
Our duo, an advance party gone ahead
Into the bewilderness where snipers lie;
What hurts is what hits us when we think

Too much of what won't ever be, before we die.
I must try, my love, I must try
To reach the foxhole where we can resupply;
Hold on to our single bodies, and know heroic touch
Doubles up all effort, and is much, is all.

June 2018

7/7/18 – PEMBROKE TO LONDON

Statements do half the work of imagination;
Claim, counter-claim, verify, but in the still,
Hot train, so-called time is only an interval;
Heat a kind of local sun, pin-pointing off.

Crosses are where the universal dead lie
Who gave their minds also to an evening
Without any sound. Open the chapel door,
Marvel at the cool green air, the bare stage

That made Jesus Jones perform for eternity;
Drunk climbers thinking of Coleridge or I.A.
Richards edge out onto the goat-clad ledges
Where the craggy mountains become rarefied.

Veer now over clattering logic and footing,
To a tropical decline, a hammock, arguably.
Picture one or three ill-shaven, sipping mocktails,
Drenched in second-hand ennui. No one really

Is destined to be that Rimbaud, without work.
Tennis nets, and the need for waistcoat sweat.
There's a certain demonic velocity on loan,
At the shoe shop's stall; little footfall, it is dying.

Going bankrupt feels like falling, only more so.
Who has the aptitude of a god, business acumen
To reach for heaven like lofty Tennyson did?
Few if any ignite the cockatoo's extracurricular

Shades into a crazy bloom to start a new trend.
It's all circular, imagined way we speak, fan out,
Making things appear here, messy, unfeathering
As waves break one upon the next in a station.

Todd Swift
was born in Montreal,
Quebec on Good Friday in 1966.
He has had over ten full collections of
poetry published since he started writing
seriously in 1984, as well as numerous
pamphlets. The former Oxfam poet-in-
residence, he has been the director of
Eyewear since 2012, and has edited or
co-edited over two dozen poetry books.
A Canadian who became British, he
also converted to Catholicism while
living in England. Still he finds faith a
fragile thing, which he does not nurture
properly. He is married to an Irish
barrister. He loves animals, especially
cats. His PhD is from UEA and explores
style in mid-century British poetry.
He is Poet-in-residence for Pembroke
College, Cambridge University
for a year, September 30, 2017 –
September 30, 2018.